IF NOT METAMORPHIC

AHSAHTA PRESS

The New Series

NUMBER 32

IF NOT METAMORPHIC

BRENDA IIJIMA

AHSAHTA PRESS

BOISE STATE UNIVERSITY • BOISE • IDAHO • 2010

Ahsahta Press, Boise State University
Boise, Idaho 83725
http://ahsahtapress.boisestate.edu
http://ahsahtapress.boisestate.edu/books/iijima/iijima.htm

Library of Congress Cataloging-in-Publication Data

Iijima, Brenda.
If not metamorphic / Brenda Iijima.
    p. cm. -- (The New series ; no. 32)
ISBN-13: 978-1-934103-10-4 (pbk. : alk. paper)
ISBN-10: 1-934103-10-1 (pbk. : alk. paper)
I. Title.
PS3559.I35I36 2010
811'.54--dc22

                              2009019149

ACKNOWLEDGMENTS

Thanks to Evelyn Reilly for her careful reading and insightful commentary and to
Jill Magi for her thoughtful conversations regarding this text. I am grateful to Tom
Fink for his intense critical engagement with *If Not Metamorphic?* in chapbook
form. Thanks as well to Peter Gizzi, who selected this book as the runner-up for
the Sawtooth Award.

Sequences from this book have appeared in the following places: *The Brooklyn
Rail*, Mónica de la Torre, editor; *Dusie*, Susana Gardner, editor; *Primary Writing*,
Phyllis Rosenzweig and Diane Ward, editors; *Tool a Magazine.com*, Eric Sweet and
Vincent Sweet, editors; *Xantippe*, Kristen Hanlon, editor.

THIS BOOK IS DEDICATED TO TOSHI IIJIMA

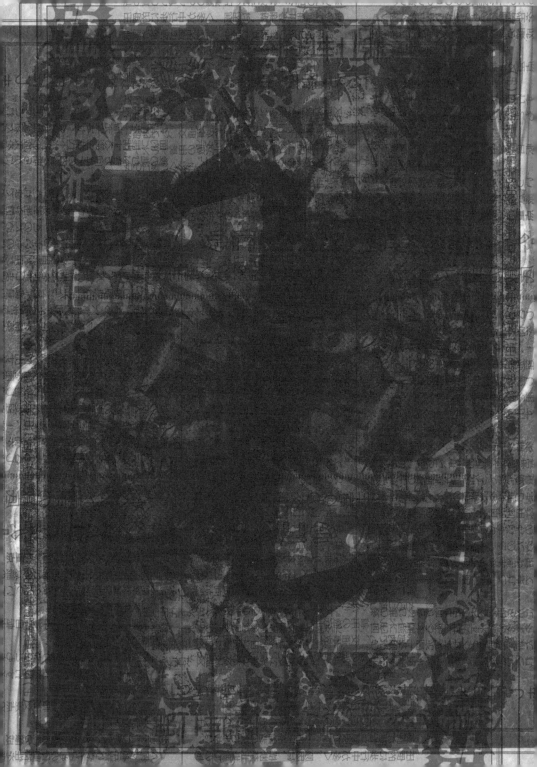

CONTENTS

IF NOT METAMORPHIC?   1

TIME UNIONS   21

TERTIUM ORGANUM   49

PANTHERING Φ 107

IF NOT METAMORPHIC?

both of these count as substituents

2.

215 +

249 bottle

215 + 10 (one

22 bottle

215 + 3

2 × 5 (two

= 255

(d)

215

RX $\xrightarrow{h\nu}$ R· + X·

RX + X· $\longrightarrow$ R· + X$_2$

2R· $\longrightarrow$ R-R

The brown is due to Br$_2$, the violet to I$_2$.

3. CH$_3$OH

Said?

The deep sea?   A deluge?

        Anticipation?

The ever-present   dancing machines

        lunge?

                Threatened to kill you?

Designed by whom   Designed by whom

        Terrarium?

Departure it seems,   doesn't it

        By the roadside?

Threaten to kill   you?

        Designed by whom

        Departure it seems,

        doesn't it

A soft, green, beautiful mountain?

The strangling, like anger?

One nude war?   Kelp?

Illusionary?   Encloses   the   neck?

        Kelp?

A snake was circling?

Made virtual?

Made virtual by design?

Threatened   to   kill—design

Threatened to kill?

Would
Would this be syncopated
slowly?

In the greatest country?
Threatening a soft, beautiful mountain?
Designed to be held in the hand? Hand
held? Will it   securely?
Designed to hold 400 pounds? Will it hold
this weight   securely?
Is that what you meant,
design

You did that?   War?

Thwarting the mind?

Did?

With?

The

State   (said what?)

of the heart?

~

State?

Since dawn

of time?

Time?

Time?

Virtual, like anger?

      Whittled down, like time?

      Whittled down

      In this country?   By whom

      Whittled down?   Was the paper?

      Encasement?   The country?

Disturbs your head?   Disturbing your

departure at the window?   To that country?

Was a

death's head?

Was a bluish and deep sea?

Was a hammer noise?

Would hold 400 pounds securely

Like hunger?

~

Weary of hunger?
Weary of excess?
They are, in that country, in this country?
When you're writing

      go

within me?

      Lightly?

Writing surrounds   the

accretion? Me?   baby's

breath?   The splendor of a faded

bouquet? Still

life?

Propped on a stolid/solid table?   A

component?

A 24-hour manned booth of squalor?   Of

consequence?

And squalor?

As the train pulls away?

Mercurial?

~

A case of streaked walls and echo

chambers?

Dirt, sludge, residual grime?

Kelp, dripping of sea water?

The accoutrements evermore florid

in a green subterraneous forest?

Throat choker titanium—high-ticket item?

Made relevant by expenditure?

6

                That
nomenclature   dollar   sign
Bruises? Is she robust, wholehearted?
Supine?
Destiny, by the snake? Does your destiny
change
events   Worldly?
By the trouble—
vertebrae? What you might lose
in a hero?
Rescind this pledge?
For me, the psyche?
Serotonin, dopamine and norepinephrine
There is tremendous?
If you please?
A chamber, alcoved—settled there:
nestled like death?   Huh   Can you herd
me   Hear me?
Like a hero?
Hampers orphic refrain?
Glistening steel poles hamper a
commute?
Rock? The fluids?
A case of relevance
            evermore?
My bouquet of ideas in accretion?

                                        For the
                                        people?
Still lives, like ideas   positioned   on   a
table?

For   a

mirror to view?

Domestic?   A   case   of   chamber-like
domestication? A best
effect?   Terrestrial
       gesture? Replete?
Poufs of baby's breath and the succulent
bride's maids?
The booth of the squalid countenance
pulls away,   does   it not
       does it not pull away.
Carriage, a horse's determination—you
put yourself?

Out

on   a

limb?

For real?

Florid drama?

An echo

chamber?

The splendor of nomenclature for?
For an alcove of death?
       The fetus's hippocampus?
              Confer(s) a life sentence?
As the shock continues?   You
want out?
Are you sure.   Essence?
Everyday
lives?

~

In a spectrum?
Axial and equatorial?   Rapidly seen?
Because you
care? They care? The peaks, the peaks are
separated, separated
by you? Doublets? To be observed?

The sociologists?

Lovers?

What to do with this information?
The feelings?
Their feelings? Your journal of Jurassic
fruits? In pertinent order?   As in these by-
gone still lives:

        Rotten kelp dripping of
        sea   water,   the sea
        urchins, their   black
        spikes, drooping octopi,
        the   cunning sharks,
        black-purple   ink of the
        squid—kelp   encircling
        your neck?
        Or, for instance
When I was beaten?
When they were beaten?
Beaten to the ceiling?

~

The hard   simulacral
way is the easy way?   Hard?
The easy
way is hard, easy?   You   get
results? A skating satisfaction?   Less
remorse?   Knee   to   knee   or   kenning   for
versification?   Embedded   in   music?
Sounds of the swamp?
        Oblivion? In a stage of revolt?
                By   now   the   hard
way
Overriding?   Thrush
sounds? A small, delicate bird? Is in the
way of their garden?   Forlorn?   Whimsy?
        Wistful?   Fistful?
This fluid way of thinking?
        Foreshortening?
        The significance of a white handkerchief?
        So that the organism will survive?
        Total annihilation in an expanding universe?
        How we learned this?
        The smoldering?
        Embossed by sound? The sounds of joy
        emitted from your lips, your limbs, the
        well deep inside you?
        Are you there   There for the taking?
        Will this curb envy   A female signal?
        To give joy?

Soignée? Simplify? An assassination?
Our   ramparts,   the   now   encapsulations,
entomology? Buzzing?   Basking?

~

In   the   greatest history?   I (they were/are)
was   that   delicate   (beaten)   bird
(population)   beaten   to   a   history   (by   a
dominant culture)   bruised   by   the
floodlights   of   inspection   the   belligerent
rank   and   file   of   monstrous   power as in
this   example   a   mere   dwelling didn't you
walk with me   Didn't you embrace me
with   all of your compassion and what
follows such expression   Was evidently longing?
Didn't   the   history   overwhelm   The   uranium?
The rumpled stump and sports for limbs?   The
shackles? Again, by history? In the greatest history, are
there   not players—floodlights
gushing   over the sports   field   there   are no
more players Who   is   tangent   to   whom.
And when. In the field? If I were you?   In a
history? If you were   the occupied?
Contracts? Billions   trillions?   More than life?
More than living?   As in living? Have any
effect? One single second? And belief, where does belief
come in. The baby is crying? In one single act? One
single secondary motion? Think before doing?   The
humans?   Oil, water, air? Lucky humans? Do

you need these before I take them (you). As is thought?
Mutually exclusive? Like history? Like history here? See
this scroll? A smelly, rotting piece of kelp dredged from
the sea. Any other—the language? Your vacuum? And
the embedded contradictions? There are no contradictions
possible? Ever? The beautiful sun? A teacher told us?
Looking into your eyes?   How this floors me
My love for   you   in   togetherness   to
follow To be overwhelmed   the ecstasy   fullness
and   emptiness   a   tinting?
Cherish? Embellish? Gorge? Succor? The greatest of
intimacies?

                       Our   present   condition?
Trawling   killing   silencing   squelching   eating   ending
Ending ending revolving feeling melting being? If you
were just to look out of the window from the bedroom?

~

Outmoded   you   think   this   theory is
outmoded?
But we breed this theory
tirelessly, don't we.

~

Medea's fury?
The   obstinacy   of   Montaigne's   Gascon women
who "would sooner . . . bite   into hot iron
than let   go   their bite of an opinion they had

conceived . . . "   That text

few supplicants would read?

You have a copy? May I borrow

your copy   My whole mind

set forth to embrace this attitude

As in mountain climbing

As in swimming endlessly

in the total ocean

Alone

with the creatures

in the total ocean

totally?

The portrayal

prompts a discussion

about such theories?

You would have it?

With the help

of mediation

With   the   assistance

     of indestructible love?

                         Complying

     with love   A result

     Love

     then

attainment

Another ideal

called Pratyekabuddha

The solitary awakened one

From this point of view

The needing of you

The revelations of forest

The harmony of the forest creatures

Though they do need to kill each other

and eat each other

however occasionally

without fiction

in direct experience,

is this the message?

These reactions are analogous

to those of carbonyl

compounds to a great extent,

as you can see from a list

on the next page—that page wasn't

missing, was it. Was it now

did you wonder. Wonder about

indestructible truth?

What does the mirror   image

        show.

Pedigree logic?   A flailing opinion pared down

in the mode of an onion?

A chiseled theory notorious in these parts

because it starts with a Roman

notion of infinity or particularly up front

personalities staged as signs so this could

be written as:

``z+(}}{{}+z all over a plate of glass

the size of a compact disc—they have

them in all of the best stores, don't they.

You'll take it from here, won't you.

By way of the Trans-

Siberian railroad is the Underground

Railroad still in use, yes,

people make

their way here on foot or hop a boat or escape from here

which proves to be most arduous, doesn't it.

``````````''''' <<<<YYYYY^^%_____ '

"~~~~~~ "Greater or equals?"

-------------uuuu/3333/nnnnn/~~~~~>>>>>>>>

        Descriptive?

It is for you to make sense of?

A numerical riddle?

Replacing other propositional forms? If I

sit in this seat

what will become of me.

At the inquisition?

At the football game?

At the election?

Will you consider then, an observation

by Hannah Arendt

Just for me?

Just

now? While

we have the time?        Please?

As only in passing? Will you listen?

Followed by a tale told from the lips of

Shahrazad?

*The Fable of the Donkey, the Ox and*

*the Farmer?*


Soft toys called laws? You know of them?
``````````

My father?
        Fodder?
                Mothering?   King?

                Naturally?   Season?
        The turban?   The chemise?

                Loitering?   Wander?
                Philosopher?   Foil?

                        A compliment?   Inexplicable?
                Trove?   Join?

Naturally   loitering   join   the father the
fathering an   inexplicable   wandering   my father
a compliment   naturally   the king with   the
turban our   trove with   our treasure   with
this   we   join in an indestructible   truth
the size of a season   We foil,   we?

~

Bliss   conscious   illusion genuine goal
        Golden sword   one single
goldfish   the elephant wading pool
A wise monk made of pure gold   total   absorption
        queen of ecstasy   Lord   Krishna
over one shoulder   is he chanting
    "YES? YES? YES? YES? YES? YES? FOREVER?
FOR

EVER FOR

EVER

EVER?

IS?

FOREVER?

THIS?

The "we"?

POSSESSIVE?

YOUR LOVE?

YOURS TRULY,?

MELTING?

THE WITCH?

SHE IS MELTING?

THAT IS WHAT WATER CAN DO?

TO A WITCH? IN TOTO?

VANISHING ECHO FELL HEAVY?

AGAIN?

Oh's lose warmth

?

O lonely

?

Ok

?

Openings?

Closer to difficulty?

"Maw of negation . . . looms"?

~

Her gestures were devoid

of sexuality?   A sauntering dance quite

sea-like?

Icelandic

with the swan around her neck?   She is

alive?

       Vespertine   and   harp?   Teeth   not

meted?   Not meted—banal?

       A   stringent   chord.

Darth of   (?)

       The planet   (?)

       The hilly scrubby gorge

       (?)

       Where we the people live?

       That is where we heard her?

       Crenellations

       (?)

       The one evocative feather

(?)
A bodice of birch
and candidly?

Ice
is nice
in sound?
Arctic
The tectonic
and synchronic
Melody pop   ether?
Were one to parody this sound
the Siamese connection would falter? Again?
Great swan? The you with the downy feathers,
please swim to this side of the lake, would
you not. I bid you
Do I not bid you, I rely on the currents, I
do?
I bid you?
Do I not bid you.

Exposure?

You'd hope for the personal shift? A
tease, stripping the elements, left with
nude fractals? Am titillation? Am sofas of
titillation on display? Totemic? Tectonic?
Quenches?
The alloy
because I am made of you

Made what of you?

Intrinsic?   So it becomes me?

To touch   tremolo?

The personal   falsetto?

What honey

You don't prefer glass now, do you

Pepper am titillation?

The aforementioned glass?

You opt for the metamorphic?

A fossilized will?

A sort of chipped permanence?

As I become you?

Great swan

You who are

the great swan?

Eureka

or death?

Dramatic

flesh?

Past equatorial lines?

Once and for all?

One

and for

all?

TIME UNIONS

The figure is migratory
　　　　—NICOLE BROSSARD

This huge convex of fire, outrageous to devour,
immures us round
　　　　—JOHN MILTON

light a war to
walk fearlessly
darkness was possible
possession
　　　　—ALICE NOTLEY

the path remains defective perfect, something out of something
temporary permanent seemingly mythological turned egocentric
logopoesis, plays empire, almost real, institutionalized salvation,
arrested development
　　　　—KARI EDWARDS

walking me through a public womb, walking through a political bedroom
　　　　—AKILAH OLIVER

Factory

stands still

outside

cool dawn

there

finds

applicable

graffiti

One smoke stack

glanced back

ventricle of

village

trapped

in each

watershed

singling out

the sun

Tear

drops

tear the wire

fertilize

fire

finish

universe

of

course

Worse

off

oblivion

obvious

                              engenders

                              cislunar

                              trajectory

Vertebrae

                              reverberate

                              drums,

                              ample

                              containers

Clairvoyance

                              shiver

                              neutral

                              Switzerland

                              odd

                              totter

                              odder

                              martyr

                              Togo

                              to go

                              coup

Insular

                              angular

                              anger

                              weekend

                              schedule

                              instead,

                              operational

                              deckhouse

                              fire

Brief tatters

                              clock:

                    inscrutable

                    target

                    time:

                    building

                    block

                    pinging

                    frayed

                    Imaginarily

                    outback

Push

                    modern

                    fever

                    carry

                    intact

                    formal

                    action

                    klepto

                    cratic

                    selenodetic

                    war

                    for however

                    many

                    days

Battle a

                    Wounded

                    Knee

                    broke

                    treaty

                    wound

                    video

                    rewound

                    denuded

                    a receipt

                    We owe

                    Rearm

                    atro

                    city

                    country

To judge

                    from the

                    lips

                    la-

                    de-

                    da

                    doe

                    ray

Fraternal

                    thickening

                    guys

                    guise

                    muslin

                    flags

                    insisting

                    stiffly

                    phallic

I

                    didn't

                    say

                    I didn't

                    like it

or
autoerotic
slick
pretty
rock
padded
forests
quavering
river

Mechanicality

strips
exalts
digital
relic
volcanic
eruption
deception
island

Obvious

oeuvres
butt up against
crime
combine
attitude
paper

The gauge

is made
to quench
thirst
allotrope
of carbon

Manufacture

    carcinogen

    cryogenic

    corpuscles

    placed on ice

    tarnish

    gulch

    delivery

    TV

    torpor

    zoomorphic

Size up

    humans

    by their

    bones

    bone

    dry

    arch

    aeo

    logical

    benefit

    tissue

    chiaroscuro

    Oh

    angels

    with hinges

    angles

    with wings

Was born

in the year
that the Big
Bang was
conceived—
wrong,
instead, the
first pulsar
was
observed
Civil
unrest/riots/res
is/tance
Mar
Tin
Luther
King
Junior
denounces
Vietnam War
Che
Guevara
captured
in Bolivia
Lost city on
Thera found
under
ash
Alabama
sub-alpine

foot of

mountain

Are you

experienced?

So:

bland

with harvest

bland with

courage bland

with, as it

were, victory,

bland

bland

council

bland

production

bland

fussing

bland

grief

bland

bland

bland

bland

though

he never

met her

bland

untouched

bland

stolen

bland

in the depths

of a deep

(bland) sleep

bland

bland

syndicated

bland

in all

seriousness

bland

grasping

oppression

bland

border

bland

sledgehammer

demolishing

whatever it is:

cities, the

wrecking ball,

silver off

armor

amorous

constitution

mercenaries

The state

would have us

becoming

bland
bland facial
features, even
sincere
expressions
logarithms
responding to
calls regarding
plangent need
asteroids
magnetism
islands
in an order
translated
territorialized
a fetish
fanatical
every possible
chemical
compound
The way to
make water
the way to
make water

Infinitesimal azure twilight
animalian brimming sail
wallow   orbital we do, we do
in the brain, pliancy

Savor the suede   jacket loins

collar

bone thin washes
lovely leggings
making love out of needlessness

                                              Reiterate

the freedom songs perhaps
while sitting I'll sing a freedom
song while sunning think

The heightening for a delusional

forever   but this is all elements
kernel carries bell chime zoetrope
these toward mind,   minding

Get on

the darkness orientation   as   houses
dissolve into spillway night
trajectory only of light   lightness
refugee status, land minus water minus

Propped up ideological pin up primed
underneath a makeshift tent
spent
your life   confluence   mine

A sky's ultimate sweetness daze

        do   clouds maintain

        pulling by   jaw's detail

        descriptors handle passion

        Handle something state of mind

retina's   bicycle deviates in fog

        fallow margin   and   spoon

        feed you feed   us use as in this use

        Expresses ability for focus

        drive safely mother, mother

I could say more

        with no help cut from sighs

        Indiscretion stretches bargains

        bowled over dropping at a clip

        largely by   and by the relief of

        beauty and   then and then again

        trees

        Striking out ships

        Foreheads, domes, clustercosms

        sensitivity lucent

        bent, midriff

        silently   no purringly

volumes   of silhouettes

savored forms

between   bed sheets

foison

Steel rods delineate

terseness' uniformity grove

aggregation dims

headlock   cakewalk   blight   foin

Simple human desire

on fire, earth's incinerator

                              in accordance with flight

wind patterns

                              yet understood

                              *

                    **   *

                    *

                    *   *   *

                    *   *   *   *   *

                    *   *   *   &

                    *   *   *   ** ** **

          **   ** *   *

                              *

                                   *

                              Polyvocal on happiness
          disturbed glitter
                              a volume to live for
          succor what's missing
                              equator, the want of
          your manner

          I
                    resist
                    completeness
          completion's
          superiority
                    a cave
                    a corner
          value life

With   hair   snipped
          from sideburns
          my calligraphy
          burnishes flourishes
          a furnace universe trust
          colloquial

          Do you
          dubious
          institutionally
          summon

abundance
witness fossil facile
oily dripping rock
toil   in oil   and distances

Alluvial confusion
spangle   squeeze   static
except revenue except
               colossal   brink   desert
deserted tanks bombs sink biome
with no exemption

Soldering eidolons
panther shards of earth
each hull I love desiccated
vandalize this banishment
heir to the particulates

Lux et voluptas
gravamen your beckoning
                                    cleavage
hurl voluptuousness
her is smoldering

We lace
shrouded

summon
Stygian hulls
traumatize
ambush

Smithereens seas
ambient seas
bread and butter
buzzing
briar

Aurora
amongst labor
amidst archive
variable
subject to particulars

Minerva
showed the hill
of Mars in Athens
women swept
the trees

Necks cleave
wolves hide
torches of eyes
two mirrors of

a murder murders

Nostalgia
camouflages
wave of life
spooning cylinders
armatures
plexus blue crush
surging up in the real
world rock soliloquy active
jet sprayed
chatter chatter logic

The tenderness of
forest gardens
moon dipped
orifice
outcome deep
thrust

Agile
harlequin
motley
rhapsodic
ironmaiden
galvanic cells

critical

terror

business flourishes

encrusted eagle

obelisk tusk

Ladders to law

raw   deals   calibrated

a cheating nuclear

act destroys the calendar

time wrenches

Atoms wildly

wilderness

a governess

surgeon

maniacal efficiency clang

Hesitations   of oxygen

burgeon

                              the sawdusted desert

the endless steppes

weeping vanquished

                              banished

Some foxy
plump future
plummeting
some curvature
horizon hellishness
sooty rain

can't uncoil
from handmade
chagrin
Tao
tosses
boomerang

Controversial
                air
controversial
                water
controversial
                        tree

Hemispheres
            ape
                the cloven
                            an oasis filled
                with temptation
                            pillage fashioned
                to an ax

The last has been
found
such claims
resound in
comical outback
breath

Mendacities
sickles
a so-called king
bravest amongst
the Disney
characters

Walk like a bat
            to bring a legend back
                  Telesilla
                  monosyllable
                  sex makes a soldier
                  impermeably armored
                  roil ever ready
                  bolder, girl

            We
            request
            a
            living
            room

Slender saplings
        thrust into the ground
circular motif
        hold tight to vision
vapor. Wash. Dome. Singe deeper
syndrome

Mountain imparts this
    ceremony
consecrated by waves
implore plumes
            rivulets, the blood snake

Hasten a red cloud fever
        bird, a ritual fire
    bluer bower
medicine incantation
vision spike

Skyscraper effigies
                  flicker glass
    sprouting lavender
           blades oblique
complicated designs
     flank deepest effect
        of black

Nervure plangent
private fiddle
wastelands in
harmony
toothed tympanum
aromatic battle song

Sun   nuzzle
dazzle
                wands
dandelion
crowns
                wound filled with
                knowledge

                Tis—
                        tis land shaft
                        requiem
                                forage scrub
                tilt a tremor
                connubial shimmying
                tendril   ruckus

Shift tangle Arabic
a Christian music
                calamitous
nerve replicas

                    patrol or battle
                        iconic wells

Composted lexicon

                                        momentum
                            ambits transmit
                                        thrumming order
                                        access articulated
Apex flex of arm

                    temples succor, temples
                    relinquish environment
                    recycle vibrations
                    solidify
                    dearth
                    a crater where a temple
                    was, ritual of circles

                            Rill adore
                            a plume of storm
                                    prates rain
                                reining schism
                            ice flags rapture
                                        causality indentured

                    Learning marks along
                    hovels of shelter

shaky timbers support such ceilings
we prop beams up with our bodies
steadying spinal cords
foraging beyond the
melancholic pockets
loitering swaths of urban
canyon, rove each alert
Richter magnitude, richer

TERTIUM ORGANUM

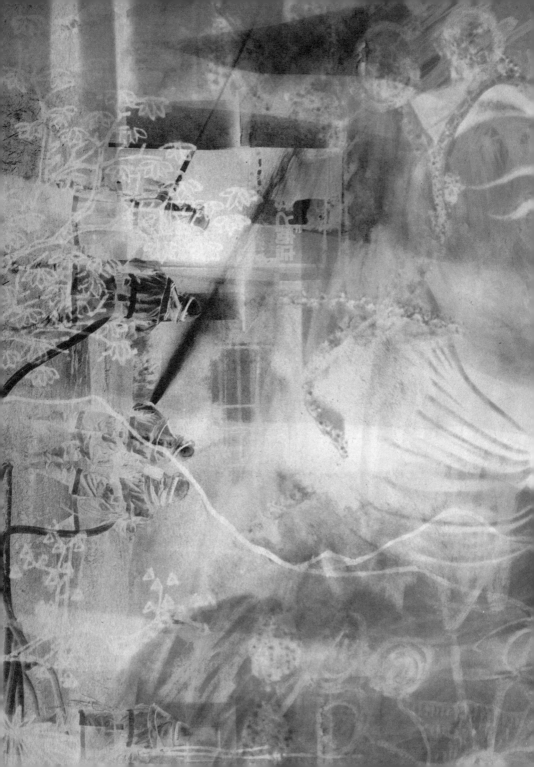

Roughly everywhere, sky
        border, borderland sky
land's land, sky, borders
        tariffs, coiled metals impinging
on territory impinging on sky
        shattered
was sobbing
        sky
skyland
        trespasses mountainous
shallow divot
        landing agreeable
island
        indigenous forest garden
primordial homeopathy fronds tableaux
        wilting large black box storage access
impervious epic landlocked stripped and metered
        ground floor up from industry exhausted
inner calibration linear faltering wild eyed denatured
        vacuous hoses of tear gas unbelievable chemical
suspected then ambushed then surrounded than anguished
        neighboring street sound, societal handling
blandishments, bold managing, such as sanctions, land mine legs
        gravity increases with each encasement
indictment

( )

        A sentence can't handle this fall

( )

From a periodic table convert bulk to quantum pressures
        Nibs laced in mercury
Execution at the planetarium where years are born

( )

I see why she screams
        systematically
velocity of thudding
        dimensionality full
of tension

( )

Spider dizzy with each cluster
        How dense our politician eyes all natural obsolescence
register fuzz, miasma
        wobble jammed orchestration
detonates sounds to brood and oxidize candor
        Little animal hides one at a time
No, mask like motions of totality troubling game
        River clogged with familiarity
River circuits, sentience, river sentience
        Moody transitional, from the shoulder, from
      Aquifer fine eye vanishing
        hungrily

Summoned gesture
    snarled, displaced

( )

Rose shutters of brass filigree
    glazing elasticity, opening
thorn timbre, catch her swaying hull
    Gazing raze easily, modular cushions
scene: echo lounge, Lakota scars bubble
    Amnesia melee psyche in cave
projected on a silver screen clash to cause law
    sexual vignette, oily halo
deciphering dubious agents of history
    Implant the guise of human rights
Symbolic agency of the petting mirror
    Mirror, the model of the lake

( )

Sediment of drought

( )

    Skeletal nomenclature
Rock posture Luddite

( )

       winnowing screed
the brain ordinance
       clot bargains
hemispheric phantoms
       mauve colored area called retaliation
freedom transmitters are neurons
       step toward
step toward
       toward away sway

( )

Our very few generations octogenarians
       Genetically engineered quick demise
Locust dust lasso crackpot dictates epidemic we watch
       TV
Convoluted loose terms as Jacobinism is
       to our own loan
Lone specialized Elysium emblem, answer
       staked out lettering
symbols made of eggshell
       A possession called light
Transparent parent product
       manufactured dolls with plastic hair
Ubi sunt qui ante nos fuerunt?
       Those dolls articulate the unconscious

( )

Yet love sways splendid adrenal
         Rapture welcome
Roots tasseled, willing shapes, butterflies
         syncopation, shelter
elation
         meadows oblige
salt uprising

( )

         fauna
obal
         musculature
wave
         natal
dune
         laved
pulse
         dilate
crag
         trihedral
plexus
         kneading

( )

Animals illuminate the swimming pool
        Affix marble lions in the shrubbery
Solicitations, usages: turf, gardenesque, bud, floral
        dire
ornamentation   shrubbery affords conversation
        Calibration with synthesis of replacement
what looked like a cell
        mark migratory route
Magnifying elasticity of distant space
        light years, matter
cycles, draping meshes
        messages

( )

This time
        the target is the civilian population
this time, maximum
        security
this time, zenith
        this time, blanch
this time, a sequel rippling zero and one
        this time coming apart easily
studious
        legality

( )

Shrink the definition
     of death

( )

Integral to the proclamation

( )

Don't tread on (me)
     do   not

( )

Consequent interstitial ruins ruin ruin reservoir urge
     canopy for canopy for coffee table
their suggestion, to seize in all direction
     no entropy when it comes to Aristotelian
nervous systems   it kills like a cure, triumphant
     History bandages the wound

( )

     And what does this say about plastic
skulls and bones or
     aiding and abetting
distances relinquished on fantasies

( )

      Quotations from the invaded island
switchback cleavage boisterous
      The boys outback to catch for camera
shards the ferns in contract conceptually

( )

      TV's silly wasted platform
a matter of impression
      compression color makes displaced in
two dimensions
      red's lame neckline
Panther eyes digitized

( )

      Ethics pursued by other means

( )

An animal invokes a politic of the wild
      Shallow sills
water columns of an exact salinity
      Fjords carved by glaciers
Estuaries topaz subject matter, let me
      tell you indentation venture what

is further or weakest least existent who
        doesn't suffer, sulfur, tablets
A drink with complicity
        Victory full of night
In allegiance why not the obliteration
        Garbage looks so forlorn once
abandoned, heaped on a mushy snow bank
        One gadget's part is malfunctioning
and without the crank is obsolete so on a steamer
        to China to be disemboweled for its toxic
mess, behold our sinking prices, a velvet blue light
        special, countervailing literally, read the
unblinking billboards—thought process
        fountainhead, something as plain
as the sky
        The words tell them about letting their hair
down down down cascadeward cascading
        The trouble with being hidden is the door

( )

I felt warm in the trauma cocoon
        of origin
Paleolithic sequence wound around the neck
        Cave in to consciousness
Coyote

( )

Under the pine tree uncle, placed there in a basket
                    The snow collected on my face and blanket
White makes green, dark evergreen density
                    Falling down downy flailing crystals softly freeze
Base roots nestle the baby   She is swaddled in sugar gum
                    leaves left there in the forest, sky is dispersing
Below is a river and swords of ice boulders absorbing cold
                    Abandon baby under pine tree
Something elemental from the past
                    Fur outside, understanding

( )

Threaded with indentures, incitement writes the harlot
                    of aroma, arenas of prodigious cycle
Klepto of grasses of twigs fodder cud or treading
                    Fulcrum throes   stowaway edges
Garden margin rows of corn underbrush until forest
                    Stone cluster walls shady woods tormented
by a devil

( )

Only
        is a quantity

( )

Map ventricles
distant residual land ooze
Twisted corset the tectonic plates make
when crassness butts up against steel
easily sidling against causeways
Fake streaks makeup
Vibrating we mingle
Directions automatically end
Imagining the moving picture
static usefully electrifies
Credulity in white shoes slowly fades

( )

Animal crew, taxonomy of nets
Pious office furniture
Foundation's plastic surplus
Incantation and future and future because
medicine has it so
Brave hot rocks sweat lodge
Human seat in the dark under birch
feels like black expansion caved in but it didn't
This could be called two faces
Bank vault natural voice in the air
sees   siege

( )

Recasts a psychic knot from blindness

Sex glistened in a theory
slated for production   I has been extricated from
          gesture, endures as a symptom
Representation, your sheriff
          To signify
an ego

( )

Volvere

( )

When she
          began a sexual relationship with the earth

( )

Provocative rocks anonymous capable of luminous
          subject, various dynamic

( )

Stairs content with universality
          distrusts diversity   simply not to acknowledge
unit, uses   cloned for complicity
          Bootstrapping from text to texture

unfolding anamorphosis
     simiesque
memento mori
     module

( )

Hermeneutics immures
     galore spur
cherry of this adolescent girl

( )

Structure of snow
     Zarathustra
In meditation wolves encircle larvae
     Murderer's other address, hunter
hunter's other address, provider, provider's
     other address, lover, lover's other address
brother, simply another, simply other, so much so
     hieroglyphic model of the ibis genesis
Structure of snow

( )

     Flag glitter and glitch
Stab stagnant resources, mine light
     Cluttered pornography eviscerated dull fatigue

Bisque forced the color of the stripes
Fathers shut up
Philosophy, cool or hot

( )

recombinant

bio resistant

nomadic capital

novelty in art

purity

pollutants

representations

thought

( )

Self-aggrandizing grids and procedures
Come into a cubical for white light and carpet
A palpable union collapses just east
Homelessness is beyond those borders of surface
Hexagram perplexed, futility of shapes make

subjects. A play on economics. Color photography
            emulating life. Do you think it is right to
cut it in half? Techno niche

( )

            tinted object
tainted
            Landmass
perched upon a honeysuckle
            norm
lassitude
            leopard spotted
Swaying in delirium
            my amplitude denuded
struck back by a brake
            the way a map of the land meets
the sea of paper
            You'll want what—
recognized whereas all resort is cordoned

( )

            Perhaps the transforming cure of color

( )

You'll need this: heart to heart

drummers

speckled stones fist sized

what you wove

mellow biometric pressure

birch staccato

ears to anticipate

some river virtue

( )

Disassembling layers

we swirl, girls

pledges of surge diaphanous, but also tight to the bodice

Fine moist pendulum animalia beloveds foreheads

Instead of echo, logos deviations divinations stems, tendrils

Frequencies, the contact

Water mixes sex

( )

Mistress metamorphose me and my

tricks in blue screens like horizons

Each object upsets

presences airy

Disclaimer for immanence in nature

wring a bit of collaborative cloth

Somehow night's sureness

so geography is dissolution between us

Dress down in awakening

comb wheat with wind as a moon appears
        A continuum of elaboration

( )

I shall be living always
        Sanction, embargo, ban, spooling a sequence
Ovid's profile on currency's largest denomination
        Food drops of mildewed grain crash through few
trees in the desecrated village, orphaned warning warring
        aids this narrative with apples in hand
an illusion, a cello
        footprints, sleep

( )

Spinal tap everglade
        reptilian glamour
Crushing drooping neck of a water bird, osprey
        A legend about attack
Bubbling water Gregorian
        A beautiful bloodletting cue
with each bite of granite
        swallow without flavor
nervous prophetic contralto
        feathers surrender to the game
flaunting sufficiency
        like language engorged

( )

Language encroaches
        comes closer toward, enters subdivision
is hit by passing vehicles
        sneaks around searching for sustenance
signs continually burgeon and bloat
        see this painted historic green
see windows looking out onto weather treated decks
        The lawn furniture goes unused

( )

Sweet ancillary—let's
        feral travertine spine, portico from branches
Within the cabinet is a phenomenon of Egyptian proportion
        Clytemnestra made of sugar
Intrigue, arbitrary auto-da-fé hell bent
        Nihilistic spectacles cause the heaviest inertia
Bludgeoning calm called hysteria

( )

        A ditty about the essence of lard

( )

Whitewashed walls yield surfaces desirous of trust, falsely

Amplitude in aching
Painting architecturally the rafters
Atop this massive boat
Photography depicts crimes against nature
Paint after all is a medium
Paint comes ready made in tubes
Elegant like voids
Felt (forces) (to) create models of shelter (level)
Thermal, thermal nuclear
Microscopic, memory adrift
Exist, exist
Incisor tooth yes, coyote you in signal observing

( )

Bestow upon the metal center, ermine, my skin
soft pelts against properties caustic, boiling geysers
oozing carbon fire, lava coiffing exerts
efforts of texture. Hunting a liberation. Cache

( )

Instruments balancing maximum
postulates, ribs: structure
bearing the tiniest types
Swimming lantern onto your whole body
In twoness the embryo of evenness ruffles
Clover pussy willow gorges
Sugar maples tapped

Cellular estates
We thicken on the reddish moss
shady logs
Many tissue thin canopies differ conditions
Capillary fluster terrace swain

( )

Coma ploy mentions read out pilaster dictated
national spastic instigational well
round-robin prescription

( )

Gleaming claims embolden levers
I swap windows for doors, art swaggers tacky
dereliction. Regulation limn
Swaddle each mesa with crudwork
Noteworthy castigation of rambling lair
Rigoletto stuck to the stage with rabbit's glue
Messy messy galactic

( )

Dither vermilion

( )

Enigmas with a little breeze
      are titillation

( )

Composting in the back
      are apple cores every single potato peel
pleasure, stomp on the rotting mixture
      Numerous numerous worms play with
pulp   rose thorns   mulch
      then I shovel deeper
uncover rocks
      The circulatory systems of trees lay here
Bamboo pleasure
      showing groin
as sexy as elbow

( )

      Pierce a childish winter
observations full of massacre
      whose turf is burnt by the sun
ashen cincture in earlier eras
      With stealth the great room is swarming
mind
      Forced into indentured servitude peacock
possession of the whole house

( )

      Bewildered, butterflies taking off apron
Worn of seeing
      Visitor of sacred precincts
Logic commences on two legs

( )

      Athermic
frothy insect delivery

( )

Gust
      fiction depicts prophecies as raving lunatic
heavy frothy waves ways waves, cyclones

( )

      Ruby hard-wired jewel box

( )

Otherwise
      touching phenomena

( )

A glint so blue I stumbled
        Indigenous blooms slumbering sword

( )

A delivery, gifted such blended awnings, sayings
        thanks for each succeeding trace
for continual eventual and happening
        for the merit of any consequence of utterance
candid leaving, and coming, for the astounding
        no longer incident

( )

To speak of time when it is porous
        here, then evermore candidly here
away from blocks of action, stuck of object

( )

        Imperviousness of nothingness
porousness of everything
        nothing is impervious
the thingness is going going

( )

      Erotic
rebellion

( )

      Rebellion erotic nodding
saturation is reached: spine, mask, posture
      inverted pyramid, displaced water
from the well
      translucency in telling promissory—*then*
mouth of words gulch dote kindle, give illusion

( )

      Slip over version gel

( )

Assassination illustration

( )

      Spillway department

( )

Childhood, flint and wedge

( )

Formations in a subsequent hush

( )

Anguished, blankly—earnest refugee

( )

Anesthetized truly, Lake Shore Drive

( )

Flock of seagulls hover in the embroidered dawn
        glows the cathedral air
peacefulness of creamy orange
        salt splashed metamorphosis snowfield
touch approaching festivals

( )

        Two texts usher in congeniality as various specifics
of meaning begin to meld. Essentiality becomes
        phantasmal. Infinite trajectories hone in on strings

sublimation of mercurial zero

( )

Tenderness tied to this immediacy

( )

      Unfolding

( )

So, among the brook and hemlock outcroppings
      wildness hindered unhindered and spiraling
dance spur beyond an abyss of an act itself
      animal vitality freely—objects are blind effects
the sun tarnishes the feigned
      nirvana veil

( )

Mountebank
      Foo fighters
Yá de l' Un

( )

With this message of self-erasure
read theoretically
determinism unraveling spool
Glued to the gap in symbolism
architectural fetish, self-combustion

( )

Airbrushed full name ozone
Other names peel their veneers

( )

Summer tinge
heat
lake's dimness loved
loved

( )

Wallow a nude whole
we, marrow
lounge, spawns trust and timber
we, lasting

( )

Pardon o parcel
       immediate land
expanses of sumptuous skin and brain
       slash is residual
every covering, coating, stroke
       cadastral

( )

       In this
conversion of paper

( )

       Sight recognition flight recognition
Extraneous trajectory migratory
       song birds gave way to acid rain
quietist of forest   quell

( )

       Under the underbrush lush spruce moss mulch
pinecones jostle portrait
       your stones take on magical resemblances

( )

Pulsating ratios

       the paper screen is torn

Household effects enjoy flashing scenery

       bluish summit of reliability

with reference to this dragging wind

       at night, difficult to know the season

( )

So it is at the gates of hell

       giant ants pushing out

the acropolis bears the drama

       so thick of itself

( )

Then awareness of the giant condition about to seal coastal

       fate. Fishing villages dissolve into murky tumbles

of surf. The earth raked

       Water encircled incoherently

( )

For

       as long as the horses survive

for

       as long as the bamboo grove

survives

for
as long as the song birds
survive
for as long as the

( )

Torque, angular momentum vector
where border where speech where
erosion, erect, erection, pinnacle
clinging to the lag, our bodies barely clinging
catastrophe feeding opening up to flood
proofing equivalences there
dying

( )

empty
clear
hidden

( )

What seems to go on
forever
as if forever
bound for

( )

       I've been happy there, echolocate
In awe

( )

       Bird telling lands since the mouth was born
and shook to pieces. Treasures of light in the beak
       shimmers from cave to valley and sculptures
theme of noise. Economic pressure. Chromium,
       expertise. Besides, these mechanisms totter
toward night. Terra Cotta. Sepia. Red arrow on the plot
       pheromones. Cold clouds, carcasses
even a horse joke. Frightening in a million bundles
       give or take. Rhythm in relation to death
Night is anything but night. Death follows

( )

       River carries on land to another as a voice does
another passes loosely
       blur

( )

Strata clearest

( )

Amply

( )

Luxuriate
    Prorogate
Hairpin turn where rock face meets roadway
    Binding sky vaults with skydivers
Turn here axis of Greek letters
    Redress spatial fixes
Troglodytic
    Penciled Styx

( )

In a manner of speaking we flew

( )

    Red lanterns, drunken war-stained eyes
bodies wrinkled. Vigorously, technicians
    segments very revolute
Stamens diverging on all sides from hir curved style
    Elaborate these leaves strewn by lilies waking

( )

Washingtonianum

( )

Broadcasting sharp sand or fine gravel
over them. The same is true for tubers. Open versions
of the world. Postulate horizon. Loam

( )

Veranda window portal
open up the main container
pagoda-like gene sequence
Your likeness
Your likeness
It is

( )

In keeping with her affection for
provocative contrasts
she brings to mind hulking nudes
tonnages of flesh
then there are the vacant textures
the gallery walls
mirror mirror architecture

( )

                Anna says
appetites
                cannibal
evolution
                death
time
                clichés
in pink encaustic

( )

                Was gezeight warden kann, kann
nicht gesagt warden
                Wittgenstein

( )

That is when
                your mother who is a man
who your father
                could have been

( )

We are all missing

( )

        Janus figure turned kaleidoscopic
turned inward totemic
      If you think she is
contented monumental dementia
       seams sewn sorrow
The cutting edge, granite proportion

( )

        Bound for
_____

( )

        Human agency
Tragic sacrifice of war

( )

        Here
there are enough nouns
     in the day
accrue reality
      with a broom

( )

So

        you have

it

( )

        Thirst for narrative

database

( )

        Ha ha ha

a concept

        where your throat

was

( )

Disposition of infinite space, dematerialized distances

        quotations by Smithson

( )

Palomino ponies

( )

Southern ways

( )

Through the hollow of the leopard's loins
          peer in
volcanic stone paws
          Museum full of spectacle and salt
Bowl for ceremonial flaying under halogen
          Goddess of wind or rain
In a city of blue feathers
          Lion amulets
Priests to quell terror
          Chocolate retaining walls
Empire clash medallion
          Methane wreaths
Pyre smoldering
          Caricature self-portrait
Contemporary crowds have dogs and cats
          Like the pipe
Performing some purpose
          Grandfathered into the ritual
Relating to the disc
          Visages in obsidian
This occurs to me in double
          Wording in the mouth

( )

From the circle by the pitch pine
hatched rock and this was power in motion
My knees were in the river
with which to retrieve a pink pebble
sister grows dark and foreboding
so we run toward the shape of the moon
Northside meadowlark
good to watch their tails
These minuscule pools gave me light
vigor for vision
Sweet grass pleases the meaning
a reciprocal form of following
indicates *in* out there
The numerical value of trees was haze
Sunlight opened the gate at midnight
You might reject it under different terms

( )

A bed made of waterbirds for death
sickness quarrels
I have to think how to ornament the shawl
Forests have no detritus
Pulverized, then wisps of smoke

( )

Quietly laid down in animals
       Russet plumes flock
Dusk is tinted
       Your cheeks and ears are cotton
layered layered
       invincible fantasy

( )

Crime cultivated jewel
       illuminates worldliness'
soil's many illusionary lives
       splendor smudged facts
surplus mudslide glint of colors
       On the rock face
hardening
       misfortune
A mining town, Nirvana

( )

       Carried from the quarry matter
young feathers
       fed on ceremonies, milk
Explanations of daytime
       Domestic customs in growing up
To get to school on time

( )

       Early cursive flourishes
express the phases of green and blue
       arranged for reference
An entrance into the life of medicine
       Punctured territory
hunted

( )

       Then
slowly is not enough
       flinch intervention
the expertise of hewn rock
       ignored by the neckline
one four five
       iambic pentameter
boldish male
       simply
formal

( )

       The first device is airtight
second device divisive lock look
       lingering over centuries
boiled down, reserved

My external circumstances
carnelian. Hard core. Enthralled by a
cage in history. Like a niche
in a cage. Such powerful
writing. Deal with the latter
in science
Stripped of complementary
accessories. The money all dressed in
white called out
the money
Inscribe new names in clay
We are fighting in out
Barring none, of futures

( )

Readiness
for her

( )

She is handsome
dressed like a panther

( )

Roan plateau, Swan lake
forged of metal, rustic pentacle

earthworld estate
          In an endless company of mountains
swerve forests heaped dynastically
          such extremes eventuate ceremony
prayer burning brush
          properly plucked
paradisiacal of whispers smiles

( )

          Motley among my papers
a reward of stubborn
          breadth bled identity
A floating world above abyss
          Cardinal points extinguished
Hovering the light is writing
          utter magnitude wave streams
may be a condition
          Conceptions telluric
Low-lying intensified brain briar
          clings to photosynthesis

( )

Curve with this oceanic possession
          Land schism at an end of rope
Behaviorally initiatory

( )

　　　　You see a beautiful sight
caused by erosion

( )

　　　　From archival vats
defenses made by women are feats
　　　　for their crimes
to be pardoned for misdemeanors
　　　　let alone homicide
in the sixteenth century was an
　　　　act of articulation, *is*
Sword cutter and storyteller wait
　　　　side by side
Supplant grace with words of grace
　　　　Such supplication is despair in
itself, or is it, for sure; it is said that
　　　　women's anger had few
acceptable uses
　　　　verisimilitude

( )

Patent meanings-meaninglessnesses
　　　　Formal legalese, headdresses
Collusion, et al.

Ever-present perfect storm
Umbrella ideology

( )

Our bodies line up as pure value
Transpositions in a game named musical chairs
          Consequence of this shows at the vortex
Jolts of degree zero   accounting systems
          where precisely there is a notion like
incompletion
          Big nothing and little nothing have yet to
fully actualize in a diary of a bitter end
          Pondicherry

( )

Inclined
          to believe
in

( )

          We survey the literature she
and I in broad daylight
          filigree requiem
Blithedale Romance
          slurs immure as bed sheets swaddle

transgressions' delectable portrait

( )

    Delirium
wooded creatures dimensions
      characterization blurred in dusk
teethed cirrus' skyward the bumpy surfaces
      hide and fur
one ground dweller tells of millennia
      Monks residing underground in the muck
Fingers and flowers have tendons stretched
      What pumps below the surface
so patiently patiently retold
      Homelessness of noncommittal faces
Hothouse fruit
      Char incandescent lips to swells

( )

Pain empire frequency diner
      expressed by locomotive surge
blue in the way divinity is said to be
    time
Virtuosic joke when to laugh at
      attrition

( )

Impressions of circumstances shed materialism
        Bodies are submitted in the realm of
tangible emotion itself
        Biological inferences dislodge
transitive physical processes
        survival, an embryonic goal
Bowled over by impression
        Village destitution utmost
Antagonism, bodies pitched for
        survival
organs based on feelings
        catastrophe's largesse

( )

Very dysfunction is an idealism swaying
        brink of corruption or calm
haplessness' corridor, a passage
        What some would call
impenetrable nature, as in inhuman
        Impossible to isolate the body
based on feelings
        every other is organic
based on feeling
        stone's suffering, stone

( )

How low can you go meme

( )

 Stone nudges   vow
Lightning red eye conveyed through stone
 Stone lost all through birthing
Stone now thought of as unconscious
 Birthed consciousness
with melodramatic impulse, Big Bang
 universe never rested ever
since
 Subjectivity proliferation in parts
of rock dispersed kernels codified
 steam rises in the center
A jouissance evacuated from the body

( )

How long perceived in a vacuum of isolation
 cordoned off beyond commodiousness
All kinds of folly in the neck water
 Cinnabar bursts into flames
Cardiovascular appellations engulf a void
 Dead ash doth the sun
Wonder about the shadow
 Maneuver into the nave

( )

Subject to time galore flight aspect cosmos light
       News of the fire reached my ears
Cameras brushed pale the dances
       where the fire was the time was
all held still and fought
       this pose for breath and flexibility
with a heart the reach is reddened
       arch to lift diaphragm

( )

Veritable armada
       Food for oil spin
Don't bend
       Flex ache crude

( )

I follow you, downward dog

( )

       The lake is a picture
the stones are pictures
       the lakes are pictures
stones are pictures
       the stones are pictures
the stone is a picture

          pictures of rivers
pictures of rivers
          pictures of spinal columns
picturing the body, picturing dog
          optical illusions have pictures
the autonomy of one owl is a picture
          upside down picture
whereas mirror animation picture
          when in fact picture picture
pictures picture
          picturing pictures solidified
it'd felt as if I answered

( )

cardinals are
          a rose is
roses are
          roses are
roses are
          roses are
roses are
          roses are

( )

Uncover meaning—
          hors d'oeuvres

( )

My coupled
        diamond vehicle
dreams of the full moon in May
        deer scrawl is splendor
invariable absolute insight
        Keynote speech
Clamoring mirage
        Invoice for that that
beckons
        Trident
the musical dawn

( )

Sweet vermilion sunset ambushed
        The cloud cover war or motions of duress
Such a conundrum of the highway
        Eagles headlong a correlation with ego,
an a priori attempt at . . . . . to connect kinships
        Irreal twins link logic to a mathematic
science
        The elicited form is lean

( )

Final autopsy/internal revenue

( )

Smallish filing cabinets ribald (of) et cetera
                Thou shall quilt the law
Paper airplanes surveil surrealism

( )

In a book where the animals are listed as
                minor accessories
then came along a great fire than
                came along a great flood
a cultural movement
                he issued a lot of them . . .

( )

Tractates obelisk

( )

                Now we ruby and blend
you ruby I reminisce
                designated for rigors
risk axis—tear out mind loosely by engaging
                ears   Semblance, a bare relevance
held together by jute twine
                decipher by reaching

bask of honey in spell
        ode to an image of dahlias
On a brink of gardening claims
        A supply of wonder
Water asymmetrical
        O hence the combination
double ratio blend

( )

        Striking resemblance

( )

In knot of Latin
        aeolotropic not drop of
spawn span ransom

( )

        Look here ideology kink
thought vibe condition, eye level
        democratic, overpasses suggest
weak mouthings   fuzz on towering
        buildings, condescending humans
tweak sweetened forks   bloody collage
        landscape reprisals, sure
pundits' roadblock lingo elopes prefatorily

caveat: a golden mean existence
Soup kitchens overwhelm banana republics
Sleeping in the sewer sucks
Prisons' antechamber opera, sadist's dollhouse
Etiolated deep fried peoples, Chucky and
his northern minions flip cows for sport
They've got militias in the backwoods
They might have been too mean to stay with the
migration   Wax camouflages
Cancer, cellular mutation growing wildly
So it is acceptable to coat radishes with
asbestos few know few knew
Synecdoche groceries
Mutations of beauty
Campaign for sliver to sleep within
to groom sod
Primp stalwart missiles
Madness' ubiquity
Miasma barometer bleak
Zoological blackout stoutly
Helicopters crop horizon for concentration
Brain combustion, neuron surge, catwalk
Death penalty, possession, memory
Each documentary keeping track
Riled up herds, wetness, darkness

( )

Penumbra gambol

with dark hair and reactive ears
injuries bedraggle our fur
a face goes wild
the size of estimation
a bit more sidewalk to breeze on
my sleeves   Having not
the characteristics of something
we could wait out   presto sinkhole
conundrums noisily

( )

Lofty, through momentum, roots of grass, here
in sienna's spine is sequel
be not indifferent to love back
with exhilarations of a spy's intrigue
transparency is not foliage's game
pantheon covering the planet's planet
How scrupulous the sacrifice of tundra
A skyline licks the gutters
This evening's metropolis auxiliary to the
unlocked heat politically

( )

With all that spawns finality
happenstance is cropped
Tears are integers of feeling
The simulacrum demands this expulsion

( )

You sway in erasure
                a tiny eclipse by your lips
your hands conduct contiguous marks
                made with each expression
regaining aching
                soothe, you do
and construe the world

( )

Blithely empires dim in consumption
                refusal institutional
swallows instrumentation
                ecosystems airbrushed over
there'll be no more empty numbers
                rubbing elbows
ascertaining
                softer spots

( )

In the meantime time means fissures
                Obliterator still a young machine
Bowled over, the boys teach it self-reflexive
                techniques up against photographs
philosophic red button

To sunder   tundra

during which time

soften the eyes

PANTHERING Φ

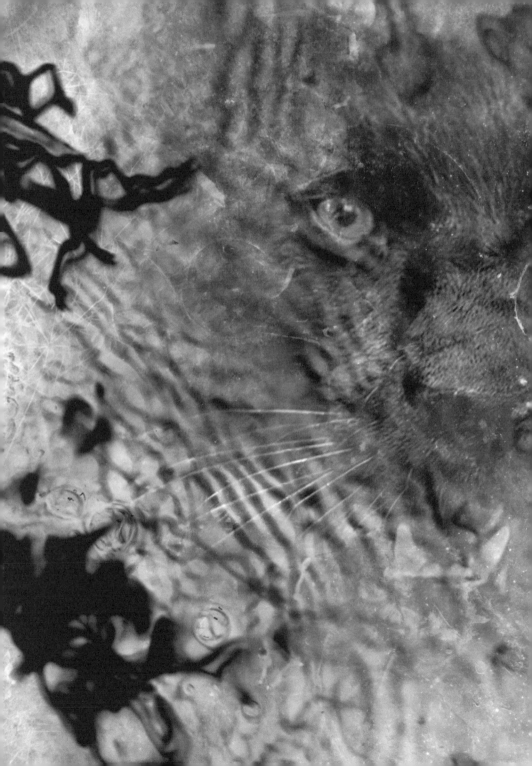

Thrashing *disability*—

—*Torn* when edges

Remora mound *where* body—

|Went was *covered*

In grassy expanse

|Fangs

—*Hail* havoc

We exchanged feline *brains*—

—*A twin incarnate coat*

Cerebellum *wished* —

|Changed into *globe*

To *spin* worlds|

Minus'

Topple

Glassy

Hopes

Biases

Arise

Around

Antimatter

Spry

—Duchess of forearm *agape*

—*Clever* nebulae which *govern* literacy

I cling unapologetically to liberty (macro)—

Tiny pewter speck

Been dead, bones heave

|As *slay* coats each *mirror* morning

|Muscles and nerves *alternating* liberty's current

Other epidermis *orders* leather

Hierarchy *subject* to anarchy

See crowns *tossed*—

Take *care, take back* our commons |

At the behest of

          oval

               offices

                    marble

                         sculptures

At the behest of

          saccharine

             adjudication

                   rumbling

                       ratification

At the behest of

          clockwork *simulacra* simultaneity

          bottom lines brine, indelible bargains

At the behest of

          plant life *spawn orb* seriousness

             oceanic tumble sway (drowning)

                 lunar tug *as* lineage

                    generative semblance

At the behest of

          all eyes upon her, girl the . . . *reels, launches*
colossal squids are washing ashore (yes, blank is the stare
of death) (caption reads, "I was really hoping for a nice
starfish"—this is a national briefing as if to say GOOD
MORNING WORLD roaming is free—beauty bares a knife
|

Genocide's kitchen

|

Perilous *thunderdome*
Action
Figure
Prosthetics reach *anywhere*
For story material

Alarm is a sort of deafness

Ah shucks! *We made this too*
Poisonous

Return to sender

Or

Deploy a weapon, which (what)
EVER

Political act of breathing or one drop of water
Cut into vapor

| *Gush!*

"THE" crystalline contractual
is   brushed aside

Washed throat's formula (screams)
Dump that here

Missiles in the briar
Uranium's child inchoate
Precipitous decent or accent
Likewise
Excuses era

Moraine sinecure

Bioscleave │ wherewithal

Fiscal ╱ tilted

Efflorescent dynamic

Illusion replacing illusion ad infinitum

Ever the while spinning
│
Found it in the town landfill, o so beautiful
Neuromuscular system was the least bit rubbed by acid rain
Ready to be programmed in a plangent way
Charge it up differential wax figure
So much trash to be recycled
                    │
The black fur coat I was grew forlorn
I couldn't hide in the snow
Domestication's velocity stunned
A docile patch of seeming calm
These yellow eyes can't lie
Like war rooms exuding perjury

Obuncous stake sweating the desk

In winter

For that matter, the ashen morning of loss

|

Rhetorical as the day grew

The fulgurating particles which beset it round

|

After that I was dead

Birds came and went

A hawk took care of them

|

Panthering

Φ

The last remaining Native American intaglio effigy mound in the United States is situated directly off the side of State Highway 106 just west of downtown Fort Atkinson, Wisconsin. The Upper Mississippian Indians created it circa 1000. The mound is a recessed shape of a panther made of built-up soil. Grass covers it. The Mississippians used the mound as a meeting point, a place to store ceremonial objects or items for trade and as a spiritual site. In 1919 the Daughters of the American Revolution leased the land to preserve the intaglio. Roberto Harrison and I sought it out in June 2004. When we finally came upon the mound we rested within its grassy contours, which is now someone's front lawn. An intense heat radiated outwardly and engulfed my body.

ABOUT THE AUTHOR

Brenda Iijima's books include *revv. you'll—ution* (Displaced Press, 2009), *Animate, Inanimate Aims* (Litmus Press, 2007), and *Around Sea* (O Books, 2004). She is also author of numerous chapbooks and artist's books, among them *Rabbit Lesson* (Fewer and Further Press, 2008) and *Subsistence Equipment* (Faux Press, 2008). She is the editor of Portable Press at Yo-Yo Labs. She is, as well, a visual artist.

Ahsahta Press

SAWTOOTH POETRY PRIZE SERIES

2002: Aaron McCollough, *Welkin* (Brenda Hillman, judge)

2003: Graham Foust, *Leave the Room to Itself* (Joe Wenderoth, judge)

2004: Noah Eli Gordon, *The Area of Sound Called the Subtone* (Claudia Rankine, judge)

2005: Karla Kelsey, *Knowledge, Forms, The Aviary* (Carolyn Forché, judge)

2006: Paige Ackerson-Kiely, *In No One's Land* (D. A. Powell, judge)

2007: Rusty Morrison, *the true keeps calm biding its story* (Peter Gizzi, judge)

2008: Barbara Maloutas, *the whole Marie* (C. D. Wright, judge)

2009: Julie Carr, *100 Notes on Violence* (Rae Armantrout, judge)

NEW SERIES

1. Lance Phillips, *Corpus Socius*
2. Heather Sellers, *Drinking Girls and Their Dresses*
3. Lisa Fishman, *Dear, Read*
4. Peggy Hamilton, *Forbidden City*
5. Dan Beachy-Quick, *Spell*
6. Liz Waldner, *Saving the Appearances*
7. Charles O. Hartman, *Island*
8. Lance Phillips, *Cur aliquid vidi*
9. Sandra Miller, *oriflamme.*
10. Brigitte Byrd, *Fence Above the Sea*
11. Ethan Paquin, *The Violence*
12. Ed Allen, *67 Mixed Messages*
13. Brian Henry, *Quarantine*
14. Kate Greenstreet, *case sensitive*
15. Aaron McCollough, *Little Ease*
16. Susan Tichy, *Bone Pagoda*
17. Susan Briante, *Pioneers in the Study of Motion*
18. Lisa Fishman, *The Happiness Experiment*
19. Heidi Lynn Staples, *Dog Girl*
20. David Mutschlecner, *Sign*
21. Kristi Maxwell, *Realm Sixty-four*
22. G. E. Patterson, *To and From*
23. Chris Vitiello, *Irresponsibility*
24. Stephanie Strickland, *Zone : Zero*
25. Charles O. Hartman, *New and Selected Poems*
26. Kathleen Jesme, *The Plum-Stone Game*
27. Ben Doller, *FAQ:*
28. Carrie Olivia Adams, *Intervening Absence*
29. Rachel Loden, *Dick of the Dead*
30. Brigitte Byrd, *Song of a Living Room*
31. Kate Greenstreet, *The Last 4 Things*
32. Brenda Iijima, *If Not Metamorphic*

Ahsahta Press

MODERN AND CONTEMPORARY
POETRY OF THE AMERICAN WEST

Sandra Alcosser, *A Fish to Feed All Hunger*

David Axelrod, *Jerusalem of Grass*

David Baker, *Laws of the Land*

Dick Barnes, *Few and Far Between*

Conger Beasley, Jr., *Over DeSoto's Bones*

Linda Bierds, *Flights of the Harvest-Mare*

Richard Blessing, *Winter Constellations*

Boyer, Burmaster, and Trusky, eds., *The Ahsahta Anthology*

Peggy Pond Church, *New and Selected Poems*

Katharine Coles, *The One Right Touch*

Wyn Cooper, *The Country of Here Below*

Craig Cotter, *Chopstix Numbers*

Judson Crews, *The Clock of Moss*

H. L. Davis, *Selected Poems*

Susan Strayer Deal, *The Dark is a Door*

Susan Strayer Deal, *No Moving Parts*

Linda Dyer, *Fictional Teeth*

Gretel Ehrlich, *To Touch the Water*

Gary Esarey, *How Crows Talk and Willows Walk*

Julie Fay, *Portraits of Women*

Thomas Hornsby Ferril, *Anvil of Roses*

Thomas Hornsby Ferril, *Westering*

Hildegarde Flanner, *The Hearkening Eye*

Charley John Greasybear, *Songs*

Corrinne Hales, *Underground*

Hazel Hall, *Selected Poems*

Nan Hannon, *Sky River*

Gwendolen Haste, *Selected Poems*

Kevin Hearle, *Each Thing We Know Is Changed Because We Know It And Other Poems*

Sonya Hess, *Kingdom of Lost Waters*

Cynthia Hogue, *The Woman in Red*

Robert Krieger, *Headlands, Rising*

Elio Emiliano Ligi, *Disturbances*

Haniel Long, *My Seasons*

Ken McCullough, *Sycamore•Oriole*

Norman MacLeod, *Selected Poems*

Barbara Meyn, *The Abalone Heart*

David Mutschlecner, *Esse*

Dixie Partridge, *Deer in the Haystacks*

Gerrye Payne, *The Year-God*

George Perreault, *Curved Like an Eye*

Howard W. Robertson, *to the fierce guard in the Assyrian Saloon*

Leo Romero, *Agua Negra*

Leo Romero, *Going Home Away Indian*

Miriam Sagan, *The Widow's Coat*

Philip St. Clair, *At the Tent of Heaven*

Philip St. Clair, *Little-Dog-of-Iron*

Donald Schenker, *Up Here*

Gary Short, *Theory of Twilight*

D. J. Smith, *Prayers for the Dead Ventriloquist*

Richard Speakes, *Hannah's Travel*

Genevieve Taggard, *To the Natural World*

Tom Trusky, ed., *Women Poets of the West*

Marnie Walsh, *A Taste of the Knife*

Bill Witherup, *Men at Work*

Carolyne Wright, *Stealing the Children*

This book is set in Apollo MT type
with Scala Sans Bold Italic titles
by Ahsahta Press at Boise State University
and manufactured according to the Green Press Initiative
by Thomson-Shore, Inc.
Cover design by Quemadura.
Book design by Janet Holmes.

AHSAHTA PRESS

2010

JANET HOLMES, DIRECTOR

A. MINETTA GOULD

KATE HOLLAND

BREONNA KRAFFT

MERIN TIGERT

JR WALSH

JAKE LUTZ, INTERN

ERIC MARTINEZ, INTERN

NAOMI TARLE, INTERN